W9-CAE-977

Black Holes

by Martha E. H. Rustad

Consulting Editor: Gail Saunders-Smith, PhD

Consultant: Ilia Iankov Roussev, PhD
Associate Astronomer & Associate Professor
Institute for Astronomy, University of Hawaii at Manoa

CAPSTONE PRESS
a capstone imprint

Pebble Plus is published by Capstone Press,
1710 Roe Crest Drive, North Mankato, Minnesota 56003.
www.capstonepub.com

Books published by Capstone Press are manufactured with paper
containing at least 10 percent post-consumer waste.

Library of Congress Cataloging-in-Publication Data
Rustad, Martha E. H. (Martha Elizabeth Hillman), 1975–
  Black holes / by Martha E. H. Rustad.
    p. cm.—(Pebble plus. Exploring space)
  Includes bibliographical references and index.
  Summary: "Full-color photographs and simple text provide a brief introduction to black holes"—Provided by publisher.
  ISBN 978-1-4296-7584-0 (library binding)
  ISBN 978-1-4296-7891-9 (paperback)
  1. Black holes (Astronomy)—Juvenile literature. I. Title.
  QB843.B55R77 2012
  523.8'875—dc23   2011021643

Editorial Credits
Erika L. Shores, editor; Alison Thiele, designer; Kathy McColley, production specialist

Photo Credits
Alamy/ACE STOCK LIMITED, 9
ESO/WFI (Optical), MPIfR/ESO/APEX/A.Weiss et al. (Submillimetre), NASA/CXC/CfA/R.Kraft et al. (X-ray), 21
ESO/Y. Beletsky, 11
Getty Images/Stock Image/Chris Walsh, 19
iStockphoto/Rosemarie Gearhart, 7
NASA/CXC/CfA/R. Kraft et al, cover
NASA/JPL-Caltech/R. Hurt (SSC), 1, 17
Photo Researchers, Inc/David A. Hardy, 5, Science Source, 13
X-ray: NASA/CXC/SAO/D.Patnaude et al, Optical: ESO/VLT, Infrared: NASA/JPL/Caltech, 15

Artistic Effects
Shutterstock: glossygirl21, Primož Cigler, SmallAtomWorks

Note to Parents and Teachers

The Exploring Space series supports national science standards related to earth science. This
book describes and illustrates black holes. The images support early readers in understanding
the text. The repetition of words and phrases helps early readers learn new words. This book
also introduces early readers to subject-specific vocabulary words, which are defined in the
Glossary section. Early readers may need assistance to read some words and to use the Table of
Contents, Glossary, Read More, Internet Sites, and Index sections of the book.

Printed in the United States of America in North Mankato, Minnesota
042013   007246R

38888000173694

Table of Contents

What Is a Black Hole?

Black holes are places

in space that have very,

very strong gravity.

Gravity is a force

that pulls things in.

5
HARDY.

Earth's gravity pulls on us.

Jump up.

You feel gravity

as it pulls you down.

The strong gravity of a black hole pulls things into it. Anything that comes too close cannot get away. Even light is pulled in and disappears.

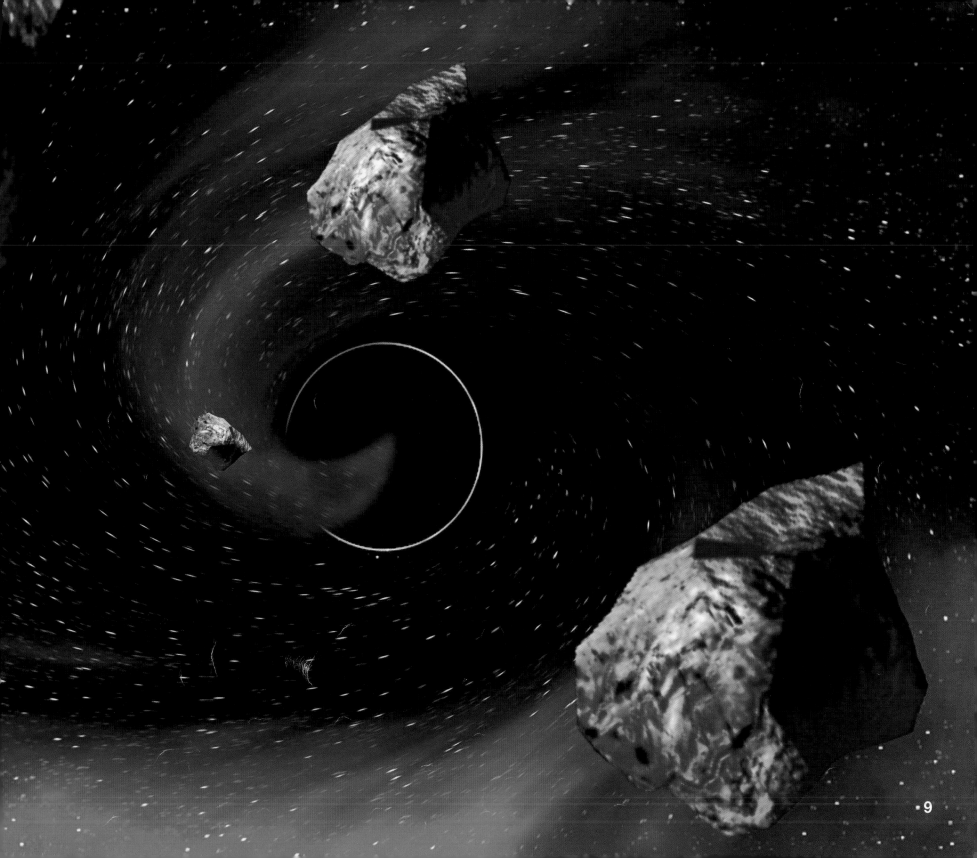

From Star to Black Hole

Dying stars can turn
into black holes. Stars are
balls of burning gas in space.
A burning star makes heat.

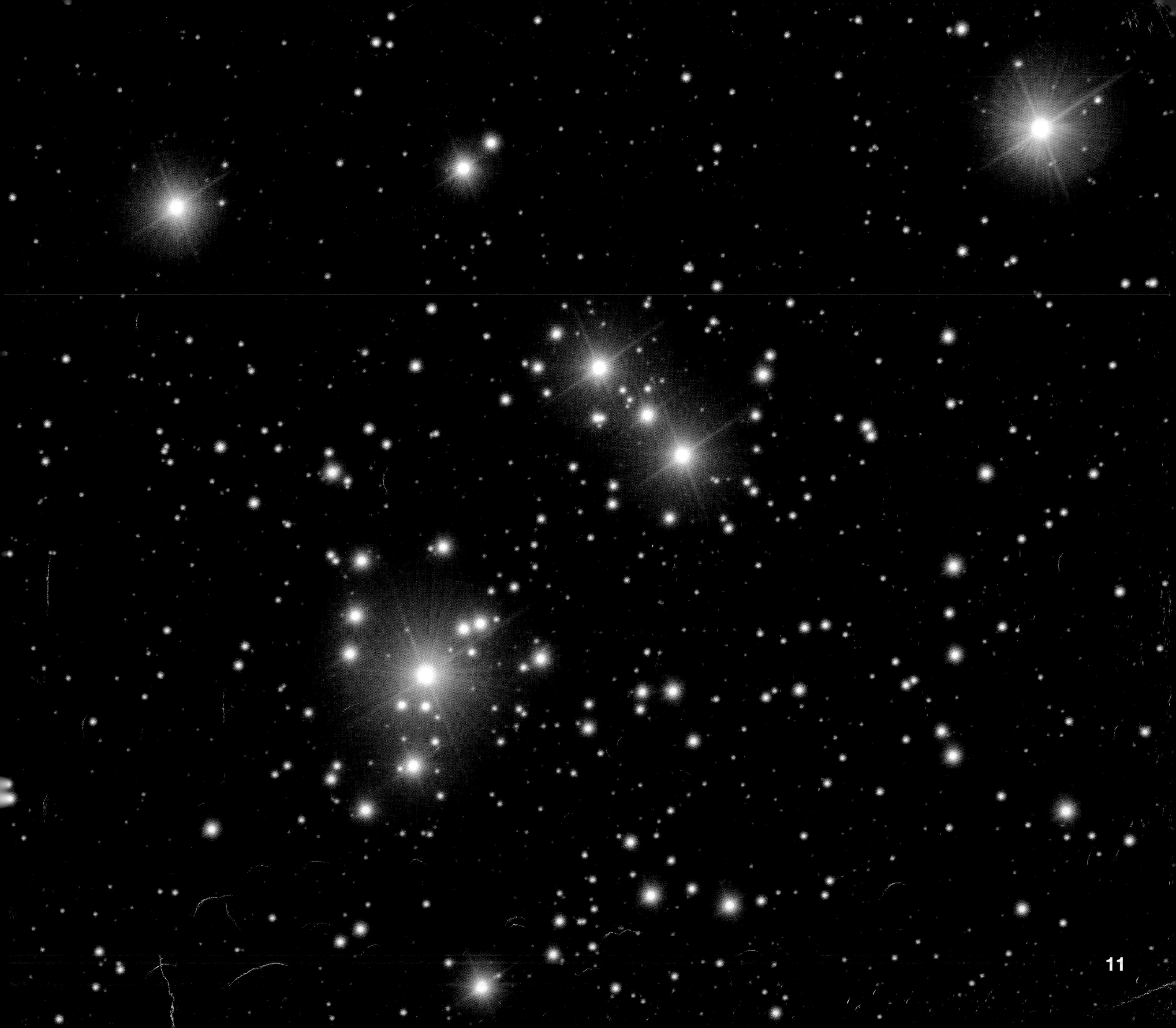

Heat pushes out
from the star into space.
But a star's gravity is
always pulling in.

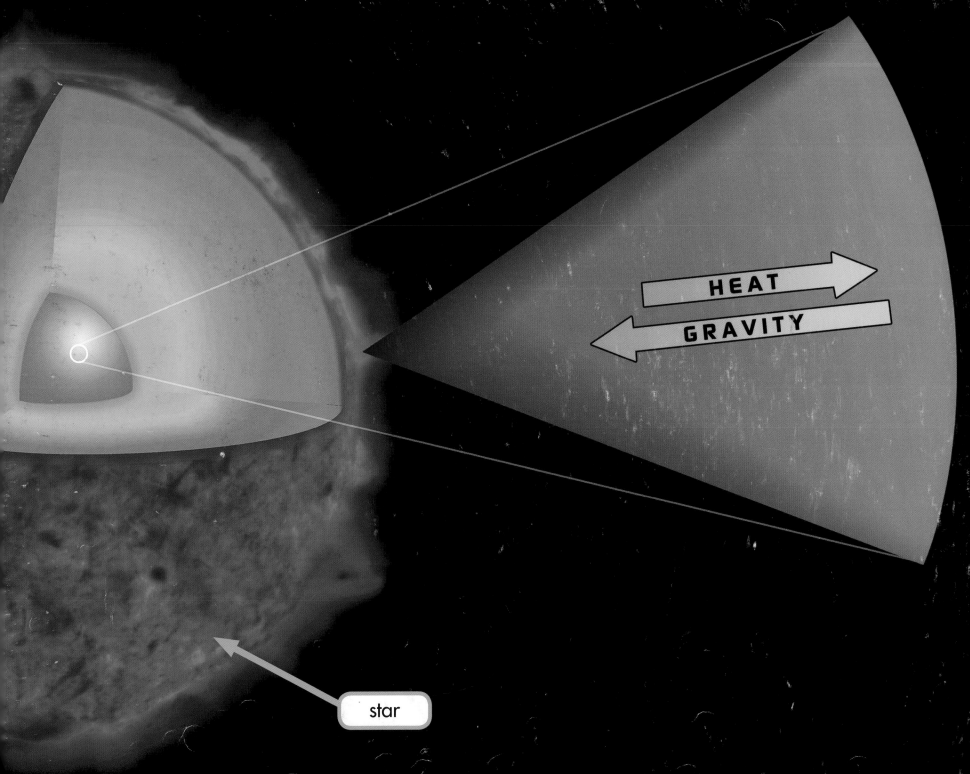

HEAT

GRAVITY

star

When a star gets older,

it runs out of fuel.

Heat stops pushing out.

Gravity keeps pulling in.

As its gravity gets stronger,

the dying star gets smaller and

smaller. It seems to disappear.

A black hole forms.

Studying Black Holes

We cannot see black holes.

But we can see how their gravity

pulls on other things.

Astronomers study black holes

by looking around them.

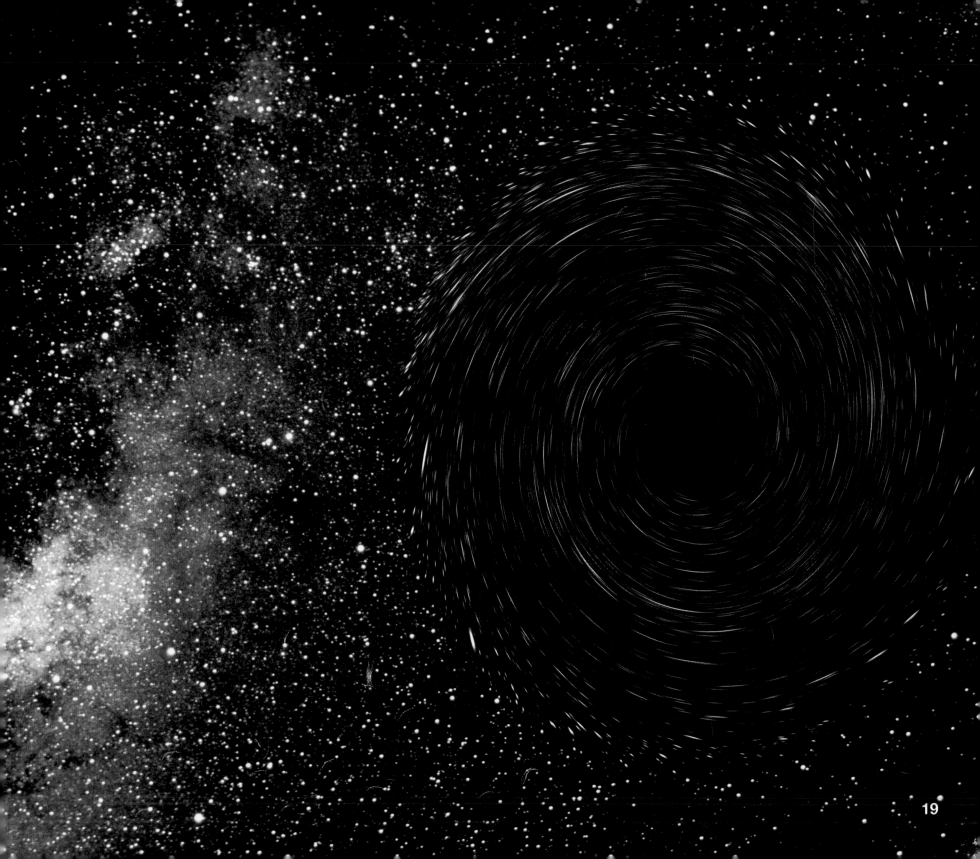

All galaxies likely have black holes at their centers. Astronomers search the sky for new black holes. Astronomers also learn about other ways black holes might form.

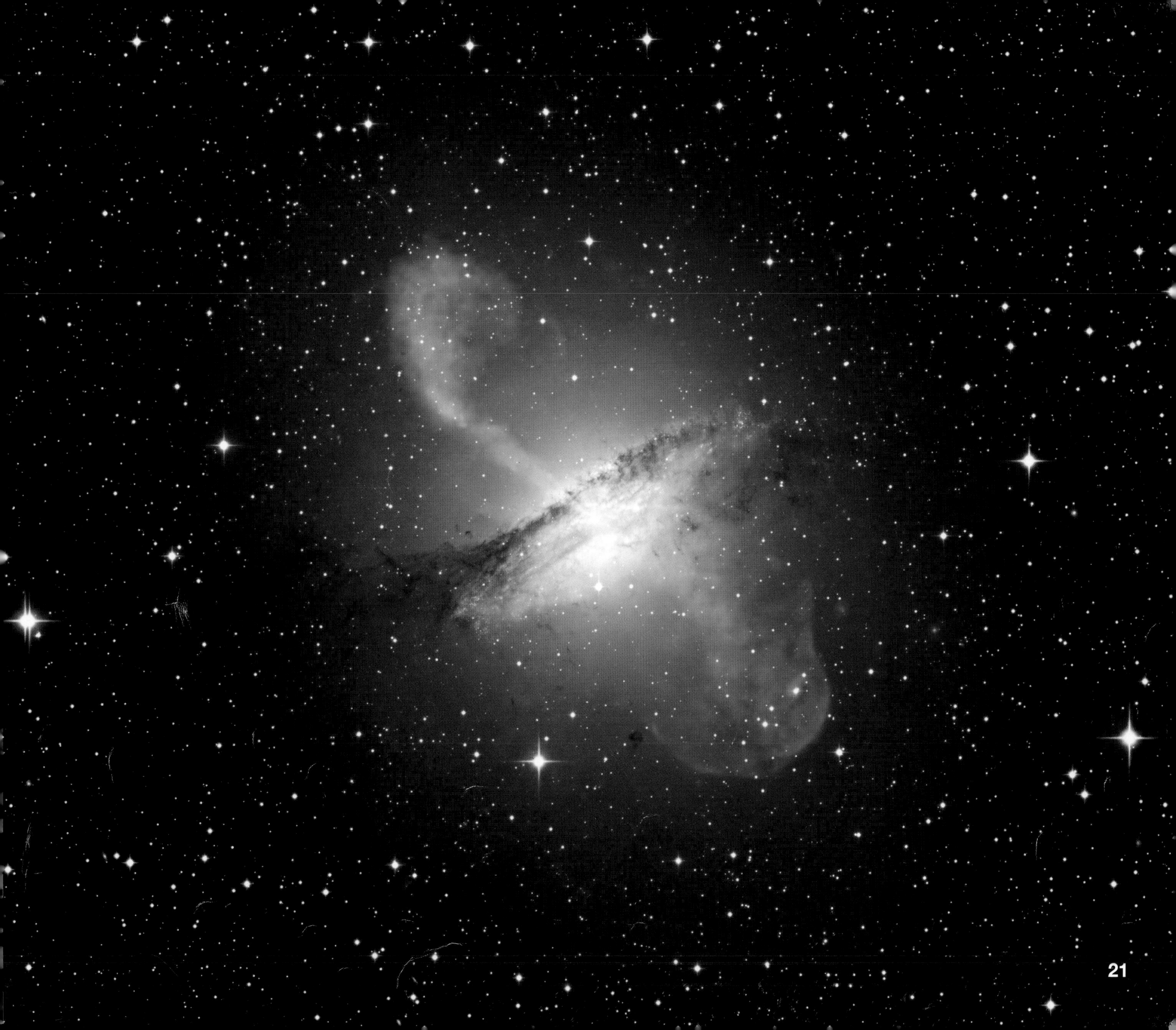

Glossary

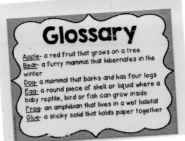

astronomer—a scientist who studies stars, planets, and other objects in space

force—a push or a pull on an object; force makes objects start moving, speed up, change direction, or stop moving

galaxy—a large group of billions of stars, planets, dust, and gas

gravity—a force that pulls objects together; gravity pulls objects down toward the center of Earth

star—a ball of hot, bright gases in space

Read More

DeCristofano, Carolyn Cinami. *A Black Hole Is Not a Hole.* Watertown, Mass.: Charlesbridge, 2011.

Waxman, Laura Hamilton. *Black Holes.* Space Science. Minneapolis: Lerner Publications Company, 2012.

Zappa, Marcia. *Black Holes.* The Universe. Edina, Minn.: ABDO Pub., 2011.

Internet Sites

FactHound offers a safe, fun way to find Internet sites related to this book. All of the sites on FactHound have been researched by our staff.

Here's all you do:

Visit *www.facthound.com*

Type in this code: 9781429675840

Super-cool stuff! Check out projects, games and lots more at **www.capstonekids.com**

Index

Word Count: 186

Grade: 1

Early-Intervention Level: 22